W9-BZZ-998

Fact Finders®

Biographies

Muhammad Ali
The Greatest

by Jeff Savage

Consultant:
Alex "The Bronx Bomber" Ramos
Founder, Retired Boxers Foundation, Inc.
Simi Valley, California

Capstone press®

Mankato, Minnesota

Fact Finders is published by Capstone Press,
151 Good Counsel Drive, P.O. Box 669, Mankato, Minnesota 56002.
www.capstonepress.com

Library of Congress Cataloging-in-Publication Data
Savage, Jeff, 1961–
    Muhammad Ali: the greatest/by Jeff Savage.
    p. cm.—(Fact finders. Biographies. Great African Americans)
    Includes bibliographical references and index.
    ISBN-13: 978-0-7368-6422-0 (hardcover)
    ISBN-10: 0-7368-6422-9 (hardcover)
    1. Ali, Muhammad, 1942– —Juvenile literature. 2. Boxers (Sports)—United
States—Biography—Juvenile literature. I. Title. II. Series.
GV1132.A44S33 2007
796.83092—dc22   2006002941

Summary: An introduction to the life of Muhammad Ali, the prizefighter who overcame
    discrimination and politics to become "the greatest of all time."

Editorial Credits
John Bliss and Jennifer Murtoff (Navta Associates), editors; Juliette Peters, set designer;
    Lisa Zucker (Navta Associates), book designer; Wanda Winch, photo researcher/
    photo editor

Photo Credits
Corbis/Bettmann, 5, 9, 19, 20, 21; Corbis/Reuters/Andy Clark, 26; Getty Images Inc./AFP,
27; Getty Images Inc./Central Press, 15; Getty Images Inc./Fox Photos, 17; Getty Images
Inc./FPG, 11; Getty Images Inc./Hulton Archive/Fox Photos/George Freston, 12; Getty
Images Inc./Liaison/Dirck Halstead, 23; Getty Images Inc./Time & Life Pictures/Herb
Scharfman, 16; Getty Images Inc./Time & Life Pictures/James Drake, 13; Getty Images
Inc./Time & Life Pictures/Steve Liss, 25; Getty Images Inc./Time & Life Pictures/Time
Magazine/Curt Gunther, 22; Magnum Photos/Philippe Halsman, cover; Magnum Photos/
Thomas Hoepker, 7; ZUMA Press/Nancy Kaszerman, 1

1 2 3 4 5 6 11 10 09 08 07 06

Table of Contents

Chapter 1

Heavyweight Rumble

Muhammad Ali was pushed back against the ropes. He lifted his gloves to protect his head. Heavyweight George Foreman was pounding him with punches.

Ali was letting himself get hit. It was one of his tricks. He called it the "rope-a-dope." The body punches did not hurt him. Meanwhile, Foreman was getting tired.

QUOTE

"There is a science to making your opponent wear down . . . It takes a lot out of a fighter to throw punches that land in thin air."

—Muhammad Ali

Ali knocked George Foreman to the canvas in the eighth round and won the world heavyweight title.

By the eighth round, Foreman was out of energy. Ali hit the champ with a flurry of punches. George Foreman fell and couldn't get back up. On October 30, 1974, Muhammad Ali won the world heavyweight title with a knockout.

Chapter 2

Childhood

Muhammad Ali's parents named him Cassius Marcellus Clay Jr. when he was born on January 17, 1942. He changed his name when he was an adult.

Ali grew up in Louisville, Kentucky. At that time, African Americans were **discriminated** against because of their skin color. They were not allowed to eat at certain restaurants. They had to use different drinking fountains than white people used.

Odessa and Cassius Clay Sr. lived in Louisville, Kentucky.

The Clay family lived in the poor West End section of Louisville. Cassius's father, Cassius Clay Sr., painted billboards. His mother, Odessa, earned four dollars a day cleaning houses. Cassius and his younger brother, Rudy, helped their father paint signs.

Learning to Box

In 1954, when Ali was 12, his parents bought him a new bicycle. Ali did not have his bike for long. It was stolen.

Ali wanted revenge. He reported the theft to a police officer named Joe Elsby Martin. Martin was teaching boxing in a basement gym. Ali told Martin that he would beat up the kid who stole his bike. Martin wanted Ali to learn discipline. He invited Ali to join the boxing sessions.

Ali didn't look like a boxer. He was very thin. But Martin was impressed with Ali's quick hands and feet.

Young Ali was thin for a boxer, but he had quick hands and feet. ➡

Ali trained two hours every day after school. He learned to throw punches and then lean back and make his opponents miss. To get quicker, he had his little brother throw rocks at him. Ali would duck and dodge the rocks.

QUOTE

"He's always been sassy . . . He had more determination than most boys."
—Joe Elsby Martin, speaking about young Muhammad Ali

Chapter 3

Golden Years

By the time Ali was in his mid-teens, he was training like a professional boxer. Even at school, all he could think about was boxing. He did not get good grades. But boxing kept him out of trouble.

Ali won two national Golden Gloves championships and several other junior titles. In 1960, he earned a spot on the United States Olympic team.

In one of the Olympic trials, his opponent made fun of his mistakes. Ali began using this strategy on his opponents. He returned home from the Olympics a hero with a gold medal. Ali proudly wore his gold medal, even while sleeping.

Ali, at center, poses with two other gold-medal winners in Olympic Village in Rome, Italy.

But Ali was still treated poorly because of his skin color. A restaurant refused to serve him because he was African American. Ali didn't want a gold medal for representing a country where he didn't have equal rights. He threw his gold medal in the Ohio River.

Becoming a Pro

Ali wanted to prove himself. He decided to become a professional boxer. He would challenge the best boxers in the world. He moved to Miami, Florida, to work with the successful **trainer** Angelo Dundee.

In his first fight as a professional, he beat Tunney Hunsaker in six rounds. He knocked out his next five opponents. Ali started boldly predicting the round in which his opponents would lose. Most times, he was right.

Angelo Dundee trained Ali to become a professional boxer. ▼

In 1963, Ali defeated Charlie Powell in three rounds.

He even wrote poems for each fight. Before one match, he wrote, "When you come to the fight, don't block the halls, and don't block the door, for y'all may go home, after round four." Ali was trying to attract attention. He wanted a **promoter** to give him a shot at the world heavyweight title.

FACT!

Ali ran 11 miles (17.7 kilometers) from his hotel in Miami to the gym and back every day.

Chapter 4

Clay Becomes Ali

In early 1964, Ali got his wish. He met Sonny Liston in Miami for the world heavyweight title. Before the fight, Ali tried to rattle the champ by calling him an "ugly old bear." In the ring, Ali danced and sidestepped Liston. He made Liston throw clumsy punches.

In round three, Ali threw a vicious punch that cut Liston's head. Liston quit after six rounds. Ali was the new heavyweight champion.

After the fight, Ali announced that he had a new name—Muhammad Ali. He had joined a religious group called the Nation of Islam. Ali's new Muslim name means "worthy of praise" and "most high."

Liston landed some clumsy punches, but Ali defeated Liston after six rounds to win the heavyweight title.

FACT!

On the night Ali won the world heavyweight title and changed his name from Cassius Clay to Muhammad Ali, he made his famous statement, "I am the greatest of all time!"

▲ Ali celebrates his
first victory over
Sonny Liston.

Some people considered the
Nation of Islam dangerous. They said
the group promoted violence. Black
Muslims claimed they were simply
speaking out against unfairness.

Some newspaper reporters
demanded that Ali forfeit his title.
Instead, Ali challenged Sonny Liston
to a rematch and knocked him out in
the first round.

Defending His Title

Over the next three years, Ali defended his title against a long line of challengers. Ali's **corner man**, Budini Brown, described his boxing style with the famous line "float like a butterfly, sting like a bee."

Many people did not like Ali's boasting. They did not realize it was an act to draw attention to boxing. They weren't aware of his kindness. Ali was generous. He often gave people gifts. He donated money to charities.

After winning the heavyweight title, Clay announced that he had joined the Nation of Islam and changed his name to Muhammad Ali.

Champion to All

On April 28, 1967, Ali refused to sign up for the **draft**. He did not want to join the army to fight in the **Vietnam War** (1954–1975). He did not want to fight for religious reasons. Supporters of the war said Ali was turning his back on his country. Others came to Ali's defense. The next day, the World Boxing Association took away Ali's world heavyweight title. They told him he couldn't box again.

Refusing to join the army was a crime. Ali was sentenced to five years in prison. He did not have to go to jail while his lawyers appealed his case.

Ali waves at his fans as he arrives at the Army Induction Center. He refused to join the army and was not allowed to box for three years.

For the next three years, Ali could not compete in boxing. He took his fight in a new direction. Ali led a protest against the war. He became a worldwide symbol of resistance to the war. In many countries, he was a hero.

Return to the Ring

In 1970, the Supreme Court decided
that Ali had been drafted improperly. He
would not have to go to prison. Boxing
officials allowed Ali to compete again.
But Ali's skills were rusty. In 1971, he
fought Joe Frazier in New York for the
world heavyweight title and lost.

Although he dodged some of Frazier's punches,
Ali lost the heavyweight title match in 1971. ▼

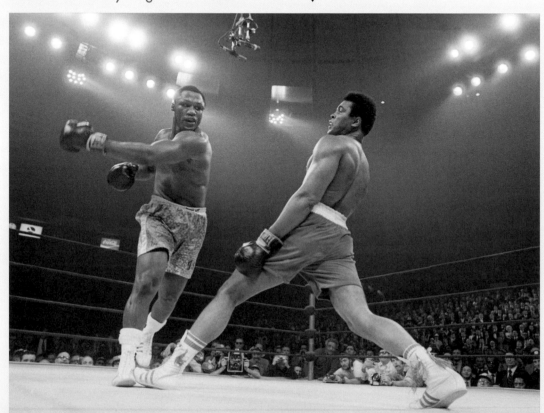

▲ Ali met President Mobutu
of Zaire while in the
country for his fight
with George Foreman.

Ali was more determined
than ever to regain the title that
had been stripped from him.
He won ten fights in a row. In
1974, he finally beat Joe Frazier.
Later that year, he fought
George Foreman for the world
heavyweight title. The fight was
held in Zaire, Africa. Ali called
it the "Rumble in the Jungle."
Ali reclaimed the title with
his victory.

"There was mounting damage that only a doctor could see. I saw what was happening to him."

—Dr. Ferdie Pacheco

'The Greatest' Is Gone

Muhammad Ali

EVERLAST

↑ Ali lost his heavyweight title to Leon Spinks in early 1978.

Slowing Down

By now, Ali was a rich man. Over the next four years, he beat many more opponents. But his brain was getting beaten, too. His doctor begged him to quit boxing before he suffered more brain damage. Ali refused.

In 1978, he lost his title to Leon Spinks. Later that year, Ali beat Spinks in a rematch to claim the title for a record third time. He lost twice in 1980. By now, he realized his quickness was fading. He decided it was time to retire from boxing.

Ali fought Spinks later in 1978 to regain the title. ▼

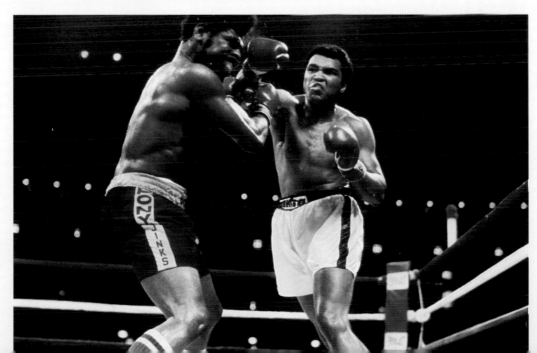

Chapter 6

Lighting Hearts Everywhere

The year Ali retired, his speech was sometimes slurred. His hands trembled. He had trouble with balance and walking. In 1984, he announced he had **Parkinson's disease**. Many doctors believed it was caused by years of being punched in the head.

Ali believes God gave him the disease to make him a more spiritual person. He became the spokesperson for the National Parkinson's Foundation.

Ali and his wife work as a team, supporting projects to find a cure for Parkinson's disease.

Starting a New Life

Ali had married and divorced several times earlier in his life. Then in 1986, Ali married Yolanda Williams. She arranged Ali's public speaking events. She helped him with the hundreds of fan letters he received every month. Together, they work on projects that try to find a cure for Parkinson's disease.

Back to the Olympics

In 1996, Ali was asked to light the flame to open the Olympic Games in Atlanta, Georgia. Millions of people around the world watched as Ali lifted the torch. His hand shook from his disease. He was once so powerful. Now he struggled to hold up the torch. He lit the flame and smiled proudly. People cried with joy.

QUOTE

"They didn't tell me who would light the flame, but when I saw it was you, I cried."
—President Bill Clinton, speaking to Muhammad Ali

Fast Facts

Full name: Cassius Marcellus Clay Jr., later changed to Muhammad Ali

Birth: January 17, 1942

Parents: Cassius Clay Sr. and Odessa Grady Clay

Brother: Rudy

Hometown: Louisville, Kentucky

Wives: Sonji Roi (1964–1966), Belinda (Khalilah) Boyd (1967–1977), Veronica Porche (1977–1986), Yolanda Williams (1986–present)

Children: Rasheedah, Jamilla, Maryum, Miya, Khalilah, Hana, Laila, Muhammad Jr., and Asaad

Education: DuValle Junior High and Central High School in Louisville, Kentucky

Achievements:
Won national Golden Gloves championship, 1959 and 1960
Won Olympic gold medal, 1960
First prizefighter to win world championship three times

27

Time Line

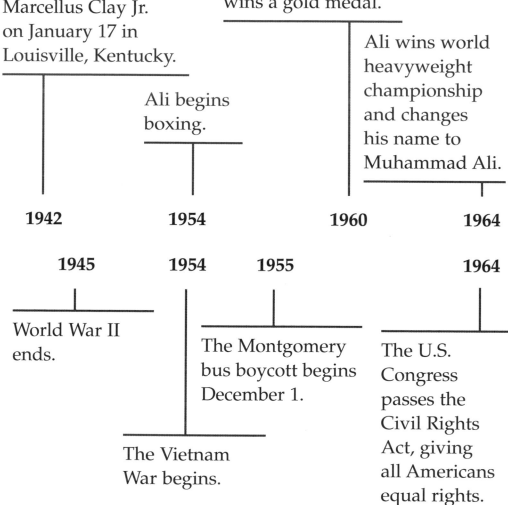

Life Events of Muhammad Ali

Muhammad Ali is born Cassius Marcellus Clay Jr. on January 17 in Louisville, Kentucky.

Ali begins boxing.

Ali earns a spot on the United States Olympic team and wins a gold medal.

Ali wins world heavyweight championship and changes his name to Muhammad Ali.

1942   **1954**   **1960**   **1964**

1945   **1954**   **1955**   **1964**

Events in U.S. History

World War II ends.

The Montgomery bus boycott begins December 1.

The Vietnam War begins.

The U.S. Congress passes the Civil Rights Act, giving all Americans equal rights.

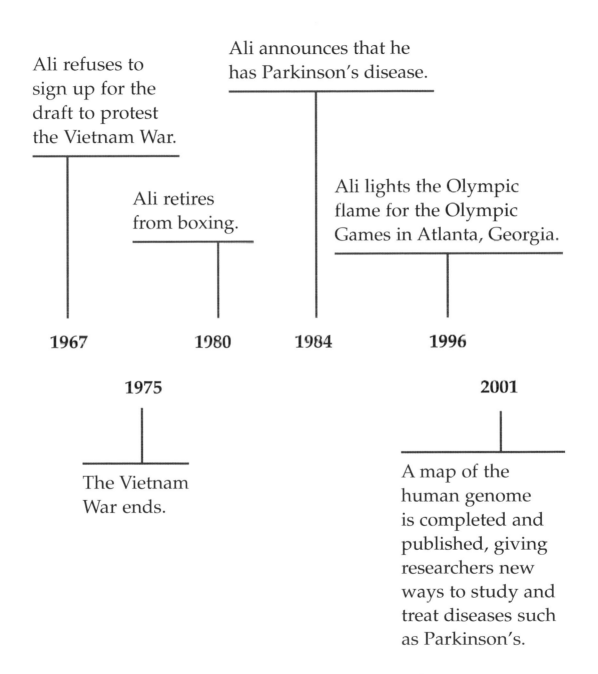

Ali refuses to sign up for the draft to protest the Vietnam War.

Ali announces that he has Parkinson's disease.

Ali retires from boxing.

Ali lights the Olympic flame for the Olympic Games in Atlanta, Georgia.

1967

1980

1984

1996

1975

2001

The Vietnam War ends.

A map of the human genome is completed and published, giving researchers new ways to study and treat diseases such as Parkinson's.

Glossary

corner man (KOR-nur MAN)—an assistant who attends to a boxer's injuries and needs between rounds

discriminate (diss-KRIM-uh-nate)—to treat people unfairly because of their skin color or class

draft (DRAFT)—the selection of young men to serve in the army

Parkinson's disease (PAR-kin-suhnz duh-ZEEZ)—an illness of the brain that worsens over time; symptoms include shaking, slowness, stiffness, and difficulty with balance.

promoter (pruh-MOHT-ur)—a person who arranges boxing matches and creates interest in them

trainer (TRAY-nur)—a person who helps athletes get in the best condition to compete in a sports event

Vietnam War (vee-et-NAHM WOR)—the conflict from 1954 to 1975 between South Vietnam and North Vietnam, in which at least 50,000 American soldiers died

Internet Sites

FactHound offers a safe, fun way to find Internet sites related to this book. All of the sites on FactHound have been researched by our staff.

Here's how:

1. Visit *www.facthound.com*

2. Choose your grade level.

3. Type in this book ID **0736864229** for age-appropriate sites. You may also browse subjects by clicking on letters, or by clicking on pictures and words.

4. Click on the **Fetch It** button.

FactHound will fetch the best sites for you!

Read More

Haskins, James. *Champion: The Story of Muhammad Ali.* New York: Walker & Company, 2002.

Rummel, Jack. *Muhammad Ali: Heavyweight Champion.* Black Americans of Achievement. Philadelphia: Chelsea House Publishers, 2005.

Schulman, Arlene. *Muhammad Ali.* Just the Facts Biographies. Minneapolis: Lerner Publications, 2005.

Index